Devolution of the Nude

Also by Lynne McMahon
Faith

Devolution of the Nude

POEMS BY

Lynne McMahon

DAVID R. GODINE, PUBLISHER, BOSTON

First published in 1993 by
David R. Godine, Publisher, Inc.
Horticultural Hall
300 Massachusetts Avenue
Boston, Massachusetts 02115

Library of Congress Cataloging-in-Publication Data

McMahon, Lynne.
Devolution of the nude: poems / by Lynne McMahon. — 1st ed.
p. cm.
ISBN 0-87923-955-7
I. Title.
PS3563.C3856D4   1993   92-39273
811'.54—dc20   CIP

First edition
Printed in the United States of America

Grateful acknowledgment is also made to the following magazines in which these poems have appeared:

The American Poetry Review:	Ann Lee; Barbie's Ferrari Convalescence Wuthering Heights
The Atlantic:	Spring
Crazyhorse:	Little Elegy for the Age
Field:	Of Serious Conversation Poems at Christmastime
The Indiana Review:	"Cheap Sunglasses" Utopian Turtletop
The Kenyon Review:	Hopkins and Whitman Swingset
The Nation:	Going Back
Oxford Magazine:	My South; Slammed Door
The Pacific Review:	Devolution of the Nude
The Paris Review:	Dog Days
Shenandoah:	Bedtime
The South Florida Poetry Review:	Epilogue
The Southern Poetry Review:	Artifact; California
The Southern Review:	Conversion I'm Always Coming Across the South
The Yale Review:	Spring Snow; Summons

The author wishes to thank the Ingram Merrill Foundation, the University of Missouri, and the Missouri Arts Council for their generous support during the writing of this book.

With love and thanks to Rod, Ben, and Zach

CONTENTS

I

Spring

We begin now our interior life, the life
of the mind, I'm tempted to say, but
    really we're driven in
    by the flowering plum, the lilac,

the early April greens sending their brilliant
toxins to flame and stagger over the delicate
    sclera of the eye, to sheet
    like tearing silk down the throat

swanned in an arch to clear a breathing
space, now that breathing's a conscious thing.
    We swell and dwindle
    on a histamine tide,

the bone bowl around a sea that hesitates
to finally overtake us, though it drives out
    or subsumes nearly everything,
    obligations and errands,

the small spiny creatures of the day.
Not that we're ungrateful
    for these walled-in glooms and
    filtering machines, the pharmacopeia

of everyday life that allows us
some measure of perception. We can see
    in fact that our debility
    is minor, perhaps even a privilege,

a god's eye warding off tubercles
and metastasis—a seasonal and temporary
    strangulation whose recurrence
    we can count on

as on little else in the world, a little luck
choking and stinging its way into our heads
    where the welcome lies
    disguised as tears.

Little Elegy for the Age

We've sworn off nostalgia
this time for good, no more recounting the sixties
and those astronaut hairdos giving way to a wilderness
of plaits and frizz and blond Marianne Faithfull falls;
or the beautiful freak embroidery above the monochrome
of blue; or the music, or the aphorisms, on the front
porch, on the grass, on the courthouse steps.
The tatterdemalion aggregate's slangy shorthand
cutting through to God or beauty *was* a kind of beauty,
a transcendental sloganeering that got the mind
out of the way of the body. It was Byronic, at least part
of the time, for the aloof and tormented. It was
certainly Shelleyan: accumulating lovers, sending
poems and manifestos out to sea in molotov
cocktails whose tiny conflagrations Shelley
and Mary and Claire Clairmont watched from shore
in a miserable joy, exacting love's price only later.
Italy without glooms, poetry part politics, part
Mont Blanc—that was the portion we appropriated.
Sexual carouse and anarchy. But Mary Shelley later wrote:
"He died, and the world showed no outward sign."
That's the part we come to now. The scale of grief
and losses that, for all their grandeur, were
only personal. It's the *only* that rends our hearts,
now that we too are only personal, private now
and retreating to houses we'd not foreseen, on streets
where demolition goes on in cordoned sections
struck off by carnival flags and cones, and where,
showcased at the front curb, we find ourselves,

our life really, frozen for a moment—hand lifted,
as if to signal the life on the street—
concrete crushed into smaller and smaller bits until
it is just dust, a gray-whiteness on our shoe tops,
then not even that.

Slammed Door

Utter, utter finality, the last irrevocable
unmendable shout, its wooden resonance—
no, not resonance, the aftershock's too sharp
for that, more like a crack across the face
as if the house itself had been slapped,
a quivering on the air as the kitchen
jumps (the pitcher bristling with spoons
jumps on the stove, the teacup spills
a maculate tear), a live temblor
standing the dishwater in tidal peaks,
severing the drain board, beyond repair,
beyond mitigating vows, forever and ever
(and now dusk bruises in at the window,
the table arranges itself for stew,
and Outside slinks to its accustomed place
on the porch, waiting to be invited back in).

"Cheap Sunglasses"

It's the last thing between us after the nothing
phone calls and letters, the minutiæ turned over
with a lapidary care to uncover the gem speck,
fly brilliance, atom of core-being before it disappears
in the perforation; and because it was your favorite
song for one summer month and I adopted it and
adjusted the metal frames so the whole architecture
of the skull was girders for the California
essence, "Cheap Sunglasses"
surges around me now a physical echo, rhyming with
each elevation or deceleration of my day until I'm
immersed in the tune, walking around the sludgy
bottom of it, floating on it, surfing it as if it were
the one vast amnion we're both contained in, and
I call that love.

An Elvis for the Ages

    What the billboard
proclaims in this careful composition where black
    diamonds find a rhyme in the motley
the model wears, and the pink grass he's outlined
against repeats in clouds caught on
      reflector shades,
    is a slogan we can put our hearts in—

      a future atavism
that lifts us up by the snarl, by the brilliantined
    forelock, and sets us down
in the backseat. When he cants his hip in homage,
in memory, in making-it-new, when he starts
      that slow gorgeousness
    and his shoulders begin their train over

      the trestle tremor,
the I-can't-stand-it vibrato, dropped to one knee,
    sweat drop stoppered in a phial, phylactery,
when he hits the high long-drawn overnote,
stretched over hushed drums, eternity pulls itself
      across the black gap
    of the universe, thinned to a wire and holding

      seconds past the breaking
point until it does finally thank god break, the blood
    drains away and he's gone, that's it, nothing: no
heart, no breath, the earth shocked still for the eon
it takes the guitar to kick in and he's at the mike
      resurrected, the butterfly
    in the leather pulse damaged, but unmistakable.

Ruby Lane

You've seen this street, or some version
of it, in every place large enough
to stratify—to oppose one side of the town-
planner's grid, the side manicured,
kept up, we say, with its other; those
streets suddenly intersecting Harvard,
Yale, Princeton in nominal ironic gems
Emerald, Sapphire, Topaz . . . In this town
it's Ruby Lane, a short block whose red
facets are captured mostly in the rusting
trikes—so many of them, and in such
disarray, as if a giant child had kicked
them across the perimeter—
and a few enameled boxes flaking
against the carport. You know the rest,
the burst sofa on the porch,
the three-legged swingset in the side-
yard dirt, and always
that curious stillness, as if something
momentous were about to happen.
But you can't wait for it, you're briefly
lost, you drive on.
(And behind you a hundred windows flare.
You glance back but they're opaque, of course,
always have been, curtained or cardboarded
or painted out. You drive on.)

It was this afternoon's storm that made me
think of it: one of those 80 degrees falling
barometer April hailstorms, ice

artillery shelling everything in gale force
and no indoor power, electricity sucked
out of the wires and unleashed
in great cracking arcs above the trees,
then cut off, just like that,
God's Jekyll hand back on the switch.
And all those cataracted eyes, all that was
left of the infantry, staring up at the melting
sun. I wondered then what it had sounded
like under the tin roofs on Ruby Lane,
against the torn screens, and if the children
had chased the cold marbles flung into
their living rooms and put them in their mouths
as my children had.
I wondered if they'd held them
harder against their teeth.

Reading Virgil

from this ledge of sun where I sit, black shirt burning,
    looking up sometimes into the wells
of dark the living room preserves, I can see
    how the venetian lights,
striping the floor, hinge a passageway from this world
    to the next
where *The Georgics* instructs the sill's terrarium
    in seed-time and in flower.
How easily my guide telescopes into the dwarfed
    dimension: If you can't
be a vegetarian, the cardiac evangelist on TV advises,
    then eat the vegetarians
of the sea—clams, oysters, scallops. But those
    opalescent mouthfuls
wobble against the tongue like sheeps' eyes in Virgil,
    swollen with plague and death to eat.
"As storm-squalls run across the surface of the sea
    Disease comes, not killing sheep singly."
And the destruction moves down the hillsides into the sea,
    taking appetite
to its demise in salt, which kills as it preserves,
    ruins the soil
but keeps the meat, though not for those of us alive
    at the end of the poem
who seek, momentarily, to live on sunlight
    and air
like the almost-all-chlorophyll spider fern,
    producing nothing
but itself and spiky shadows across the page.

Hopkins and Whitman

Hard to imagine two men more unlike, the one
a solitary wrestling in his cell with palpable Doubt,
the other striding the continent in great unbooted
certainty. And yet there was that kinship, pitched

past pitch of grief, and battlefield nursing—
"What is removed drops horribly in a pail"—
and Hopkins's own admission: "I know Walt Whitman's
mind to be more like my own than any man's living.

As he is a very great scoundrel, this is not
a pleasant confession." How magnetic the expanse
between fastidious and crude when cast
into the field of dappled things! For Hopkins,

the cows and finches and trout of a world whose
stippled shadows served to throw into relief
the Godlight, though his own scree of darkness—
the mountainslide, the mind's cliffs of fall—

was for days heaped on days impenetrable;
for Whitman, the skewed patchwork of criminal
and child twinned in one body and one land,
sending out its pied beauty in a cruel Morse—

blue/gray, blue/gray—horrible and redemptive
at once, for the Godlight shone through the stippled
bandages . . . This was a man and country
straining to heal itself, something the English

priest in exile's Dublin knew something
about. Cold Ireland must have warmed a little
when the Classics Professor, Society of Jesus,
opened the newspaper to rawly dazzling American

nakedness. Unruly America would have bent
at once to the rigors of principle, had those
rigors been in print. But it was less their lives
which rang accord than it was their deaths,

though Whitman had his pharaonic tomb,
secured with locks against robbers, and Hopkins
a bare-stripped room. It was their deaths
that knelled through their poems from the earliest

verses: Whitman, so much a part
of the sea he loved and feared, drowned
in the oceanic emphysema of his lungs. His last
day he was moved onto a sort of water bed

on the floor, "Oh I feel so good" his last
words when he heard the waves falling against
his sides. And Hopkins, spent with the typhoid
his fevered poems had long pointed to,

after great agitation, this clearing: "I am so happy."
And surely God stood at his pillow then.
And surely the sea made its smooth reclamation.
If we take heart in anything, it is a serene death

and the poems unfolding in reverse that we might
see death in all its guises, back to the first
awareness: "We hear our hearts grate on themselves;
it kills to bruise them dearer."

Tornado Watch

Biblical, we said, as if we knew what that meant,
   Odyssean,
      lashed to the wail of the Civil Defense
Siren, itself lashed to each sighting of a funnel cloud
   touching down:
      Too late, too late, it shrieked
beneath the thunder, on and on, intermittent but continuous,
   the only man-made power still going
      after the outages and brief
falterings of our own interior lightning, lamps
   shorting out on the domestic
      tableau: children huddled
beneath the dining room table, me sliding down the wall,
   and you out on the front porch
      transported across twenty years
to the synaptic firing of lysergic acid
   working its etchwork
      on the neural stump, all cortex,
thank god, the tough outer layer whose surface
   recorded
      (but wouldn't let in)
the next door's amplified needle-stuck drum solo
   which changed forever
      your notion of pulse and arrest.

Dog Days

It's the willed trick of concentration
   that makes of these heat-heavy
bogged declivities—the graves of
   boulders we've levered up
to line the footpath to the house—
   snow-angels,
and of the sweat sluicing down
   into the wristbands
of our canvas gloves, run-off
   from the glacial peaks
that once surrounded
   the bowl of the prairie.
It's the pioneer trick cowboys
   use, and construction
workers and road crews, and is old
   as weather,
though given hip status now, and called
   "visualizing" or "image
therapy," a kind of negative capability:
   the mirage is really a glimpse
of the real world but telescoped
   so it seems we never arrive
there. Mirage pulled the wagon
   trains toward the horizon
and tugged babies from the darkness.
   All the tired souls sucked
into the afterlife were unstrapped
   from the travois and lifted up
by its shimmer.
   This is still a visionary place,
though the air conditioner buzzes
   and drips inside the window sill

and obscures the sheen
   of what's there before us.
It takes outside work and
   a density of watered air
and mosquitoes to feel in this plain,
   before this house was on it,
the itch for a new West.

California

It's that first twangy vowel
that gets me, the tang of bucket water filling
the mouth before slurring out,
comfortable and foreign at once,
which the tongue lingers over

like a back tooth, *California.*
Imagine the Midwest boy sounding its outer reaches
for the first time, puzzling the Pacific
over and over
(does Atlantic mean war then?)

till it becomes the entrance
for his nightly wrestling bouts: You be Docile,
he instructs his father, and I'll be
Pacific! And hurls
his head into his father's belly

wrapping his frondy arms
and legs around him to drag him deep into the sea-
blue downs of his sleeping bag.
Imagine California
as this second language, the one

Odysseus learned as he was fetched
from the sea, Nausicaa's sibilance still the sea
in his delirium until he woke
and broke into syllables
the girls washing and the gull's cries.

Imagine this second language
in the sea crackle around the pier where a woman,
displaying a cowrie, tries to find
the English for it,
though the Midwest boy

wouldn't know it either,
or would hear in it the cowboy—his passion—
    whose inland foraging turns up
        the chiseled
    shell-like arrowheads he prizes.

    He speaks to her
anyway, not in the near-pidgin I fall into,
    but in his own polite prairie rhythms.
        What she hears there,
    Privilege, I'd guess, but some

        of his sweetness
as well, becomes part of their struggle
    to make the sea creature yield
        to their understanding
    of it. Imagine their struggle

        coming all the way back
from that other California, the one we gave up on
    years ago, before this child
        was even born.
    He reinvents Paradise

        out of the available
props—palm trees and shells, naturally, but also
    the millions of cars flashing
        their turn
    and the woman signaling back,

        the haze over the exit
paling on the water. You be Ozone, he begins again,
    and I'll be Cowrie. Imagine everything
        contained in the sheer sound
    of that imperative: torn sky and mollusc,

  Ruth in tears
amid the alien corn and the boy who spoke to her,
  the father unlocking his hammerhold
    to receive the next blow
  and the mother trying to hold it in place:

    imagine the threads
of these histories converging for a moment
  in a common language that was nation-less
    and buoyant
  and sounding something like home.

II

Artifact

It turned up as we were packing, this last nipple
    on its plastic disc, survivor somehow
from the rout and purge of the artificial,
        lint-wrapped from its long hiding,
    and bug-traveled,
but no less perfect for all that,
    the tiny bud still erect, still an invitation
to investigate solitude or meditation,
        the now less sharply precipitous
    descent into sleep.

Freud somewhere at some point must say
    something about it,
not this latex model of course but the idea
        of it, the sugar teat
    dipped in molasses or port,
first object lesson in substitution and second-
    best, Wordsworth's "fallings from us,
vanishings." For it *is* the first vanishing,
        a banishment
    into the expeditious, unlatching

the mother from her child, the child
    from his unconsciousness.
Now, he might say, begin the satisfactions
        of the self,
    the triumph of fastening the blue plate
across the mouth to keep it there.
    Or, now might begin
the disaffections, the surly tongue that won't
        conform
    to the unalterable form.

Napoleon, falling again and again at Josephine's
        breast, over-reached himself.
Demosthenes, his mouth full of stones,
                achieved persuasion.
        And arcing between all such masculine histories
the curved simulacrum of the breast, shape of the planet,
        some have said, the Eternal Feminine—
or would be, if these new age pacifiers were not
                so bulbous
        at their tip, so elongated at the shaft.

My South

Because no one ever says "My North"
or "My East"—imagine owning sidewalks tunneled under
by the lit snakes of subways, or the glass towers'
unearthly sulfurous beauty burning

all night and day, or the blocks
of boxed apartments, the sewage running to the sea,
the pressed effluvia of squashed, hemmed-in
flesh, think of owning that!—

and because "My West" is comical
in its cactus-and-saddle Mythos, and too vast,
the South is, almost by default, the land held
on promissory for anyone

who cares to claim her, proud to be
lodged in the collective mind for whom provincial
means first and last *province*: separate,
contained, and cut off from the main.

My South is girdled about
by enemy forces, the socialists who would homo-
genize and nationalize, who send in news
anchors from the heartland

to teach the diphthong,
to stir up the citizenry to bring down the war-
dead flag; she is at bay. But because
she is My South,

because she is owned
in a perpetual and twilit magnolia summer
in a part of the brain that renders
even burnings and nightsticks

as indigenous as doo-rags,
she will be forever the mistress, the odalisque,
the always-protected, langorous genteel,
and will never be married.

I'm Always Coming Across the South

This time in the lot behind the grocery store
    where we went to pick up boxes,
part of a soda crate sent me straight back
    to my mother's friend, a woman
who kept in her garage a crate of Pepsi, the heavy
    bottled kind,
whose wooden honeycomb had to be hand-trucked
    to her car then hoisted
by a neighborhood kid onto the concrete apron
    where it never sported
more than six empties, a conscious fairy-tale well
    endlessly replenishing itself
whose significance became my first real-life parable.
    Look at Mrs. Austin,
my mother would say whenever we whined for something
    we couldn't afford,
to Mrs. Austin a bottle of Pepsi *whenever she wants it*
    is wealth.
Even at eight, I knew what that meant, that she had been
    poor as dirt,
a real dirt yard that was swept or raked I guess
    like a Japanese garden
(though that comparison comes years later and
    not from her);
not anyone's wartime deprivation but generations of want
    in a dead-last pocket
of dead-last Mississippi from which she *rose*
    —my mother's voice
rising on that last in a round end-of-discussion flourish—
    Okay, I'd say,
so give me a Pepsi then, and she'd sigh and move off
    into another part of the house

where there weren't any smart aleck children
 vaccinated against
specific and local pities. I failed in the moral
 perspective category,
missed the point, but it's surprising how clearly
 I can still summon
the picture of that woman and her garage, how Pepsi,
 even after thirty years,
has the power to provoke in me a twinge,
 not of pathos,
exactly, or nostalgia, but something like historical
 consciousness,
if that's not too grand a term, a long view
 in reverse,
which sets alongside her racism and xenophobia
 (she wouldn't go
to parades, she said, because there were so many
 of Them watching)
a kind of generosity. She would invite my mother
 and me
to tealess teas where we each had placed before us
 a bottle *and* a glass
(both cupped in six-petaled plastic flowers), to show
 we didn't have to share.
That gesture doesn't dilute her poison, even in
 retrospect,
just makes it that much less forgettable, so that drinking
 from a glassy
long-necked Pepsi comes to mean swallowing something else
 as well,
means participating in her South. I generally
 buy the cans,

I rarely hit the downtown Rexall fountain, slated
    for renewal anyway,
and I've moved away from the South. The one thing
    I can't tidy up,
even in revisionist memory, is my part in all this,
    my flag of Christian charity,
which allowed those stones to fall undeflected
    except by my mother's unanswerable
command: Look at her life—who are we to judge,
    whose passivity,
the genesis of my own, was probably not the example
    she intended.
I don't know what she intended. I don't know
    if it's possible
for me to divorce love from conciliation even now.
    I think I must love my children
the same way she loved me. Look
    at Mrs. Austin,
I'll tell them someday. Explain it to me.

Slow

Do you know, the fortune-teller asked him,
that one of your children is slow? And he, stricken, said
I don't know that yet. And it was no longer a carnival
gaiety. I can help you, she said. But nothing more
about the baby. There was still the arcade before us
and the ferry with its lights. But he had answered
yet. The still-to-come.

I'm not a believer. I'm not afraid. But I write this
anyway, as an exorcism or countermagic, that if he's slow,
he's slow to anger or despair, slow to see
a mortal correspondence in those heavens
where he carries water from one god to the next.

Bedtime

Even a fabulist
whose powers extend to the very verge
of sleep (and
beyond, taking new dimension from the enemy mist),
will sometimes diverge
from the strict conventions of a made-up land

and tell the truth.
History, our son calls this, or the Bible.
It's not his desire
we're acceding to, but some dark proof
of our own, some tribal
loyalty, it must be, whose genealogy wires

the three of us
like beads, though around whose neck
we aren't quite clear:
the hallowed light, or cosmic dust,
whatever space we check
for God. In any case, we sheer

from Hansel and Gretel
to Noah to Simplified Science, looking for the hook.
(He's an imperious critic,
demanding more than a waif in the shtetl
or magic book
to lower him into sleep.) It's a tricky

enterprise, predicting
his immersion, which we complicate
by all these Western
myths. Will he grow up faithless, seeing
each cruelty as fated
as the next, each miracle turned

to a minor key?
For he's a child of his time, after all. He *expects*
        the fairy, the angel,
the whale's belly somehow divinely free
        of peristalsis, unwrecked
by its acidity. It's something else

        he wants, or needs.
We may have stumbled on it last night,
        halfway through the children's Daniel
(the fiery furnace part). Not the deeds—
        what's heresy or idol-fright
to him?—but the names, the runnel

        of sounds alone
reinventing his exotic. Shadrach, Meshach,
        Abednego! Incantatory
blisses on the tongue now grown
        silly in repetition; undidactic,
uninsisted upon, but overtaking the story

        like a spell
we too fall under, despite ourselves.
        Shadrach, Meshach, Abednego!
Goodbye to history, continuity, heaven and hell.
        The moral's shelved.
The names alone go with him when he goes.

Spring Snow

        The yield of crumbs
    from our shaken cloth sinks
in the overnight whiteness. From some
    aerial perspective there must wink
        a mica signal of food
    for the birds alight, and it's good

        to feed them so,
    to subvert the subversive
in a small way and reclaim the unsnowed
    season. This sieve
        of wheat can't save
    the magnolia though, whose lave

        of ice coats the half-
    sprung buds. They've drawn
into themselves, contemplating zero perhaps
    or the arrogance of sky. Gone
        like the first bees
    and pupae of fritillaries.

        Only the forsythia,
    whose time is short in any case,
still butters the perimeter. In game dementia
    each yellow arm waves,
        defying the reductive same-
    ness renaming

        every crust,
    lawn chair, tabletop stump
as white-nothing, or little-boy-lost,
    for this is the tale wherein each clump
        of snow conceals
    the expected world, which reels

someplace else,
in a glassed universe shaken
by an Atlas-child who, bored with elves
and fairyland, has taken
mutability
and rimed it with eternity.

The Lost Child

Best of all, never to have been—
to stay a thumbnail sketch, rescind
the fetal pole and stop it all,
restitching the nucleic ball
that would divide, divide again,
into what you would have been.

Now autumn's here, the yellow clouds
presaging ice, the mallards crowding
past the blinds where blind
men drink and drinking find
new fissures in their leather seams.
They are their own imperfect dreams

as we are ours, a monument,
a miniature Pompeii of two retinted
to a smudgy gray,
curators of the everyday:
the agency of stone, the stony harrow
of all we did then didn't know.

Never to have been at all.
Repulse the light, unwrite the scrawl
of names we would have given you
(for life presumes
another life)—volcano, hunt, catastrophe.
The changeless place you'd rather be.

Convalescence

And we, who are going to live after all,
get up from our day beds, chaise lounges, settees,
pull off the twisted linen, brush our hair back
into bright bands, and smooth the color—
lipstick—back into our cheeks. How good
we look! How clearly we are the portrait
of well-being, gathering ourselves at the pond's
edge and spreading out our towels, so sun-
enamored we hardly recognize this future, so
brownly we burn, so whitely our secret parts shine,
as if these two tones were our own invention,
and not the Nature's that saves us as a gift
for Eros—you know him—the Hungry One.

Swingset

Intruding its blue crossbar and striped
inverted V's across the wash of summer, across
birdbath, feeder, cracked stone bench,
the swingset breaks this green plane

into foreground and back, a horizon I rise
to each morning. From my upstairs window
I can hear the creaky music as the wind
pumps and falters, I can count the walnuts

clustered like eggs in the fork of each leaf-
nest hanging over the slide. A delicious
peril, for mightn't they soon drop, greenly
thud on the unsuspecting head? The children

have been warned to shake the branch before
they slide—a great snicker of tiptoe
giggling and shaking—but sometimes they
forget. I'm posted here, at the border

of almost-well, as sentry over the known
regions; the two leaves that hesitate
at the top of the slide, the swing's widest
arc that inverts the planet. How

curious to make grass the sky and sky
the nowhere—until you're upright again,
dizzy with that head-heaviness—
(a heaviness I'm the intimate of, the head

wobbling on its china stem, the eyelids'
stone weight). The children are staggering
now in willed spirals; they careen
then fall in the grass beneath the swings

whose chains they've twisted all the way
to the top in that age-old game . . .
And this is where I lean out and call,
fall into the cyclotron the nearly stalled

swing suggests—centrifugal to centripetal,
banging the hard seat against the skull—here's
where I enter their element
from that other, less habitable, place.

Summons

Detachable worries, like half-formed phantoms
    from a truncated dream,
    put their gauze fingers to my face
    to bring me out of the deeper fathoms.
    My allies against the dark, they glean
the sill's fringe of milky light and lay its lace

against my hands, gone ivied and peculiar,
    enough to slide me
    into sitting up. The room's afloat, liquid
    in its shiftings from the ordinary and sure—
    that's a ginger jar wound with beads
and not a caudel, Atlantean squid—

to the pure chamber of unfixed identities.
    Where the chair slopes
    back to a hazy cave, and the crystal
    sends its bevel of light across the tumuli
    (a dome of socks?) and the bed's cope
to rest finally, surgically, on the undressed doll.

It must be *that* my revenants saw
    when they broke the surface
    of my sleep. An intimation, portent,
    cautionary sign, silent and stalled,
    nevertheless a command. To what purpose,
to assuage a toy's chilled discontent?

What's required in this down-turning night?
    The house shocked silent
    beneath an alien tread, a draft
    dying in clammy snakes, something out of sight
    but felt along the bone tent:
Danger, this new one's telling me, *Danger*, and I half

believe in all the voices in this freezing dawn.
　　For the turning child inside my womb
　must be somehow intimately tied
　(genes singing across the inherited pond)
　to the child asleep in the other room
who has thrown off his blanket, too fevered to cry.

III

Poems at Christmastime

I

If you think of it long enough, and with
so inward an eye that all the medical
textbook illustrations become red
and blue with your own vital tracery;
if by some transforming image
the division becomes not "despair
at the level of the cell" but its
opposite—the ladder arcing over the gel
into the egg, the DNA beginning its
mysterium; if the tissues meant to hold
back hold back, and are not taken at the flood,
then you can begin, with banked
and cautious gladness, your petition
to the handmaiden of the Lord.

II

So this is how the word was made flesh,
though surely the word came after
the sublime idea, after the seas'
withdrawal and islands' emergence
with the first birds and giant lizards
carrying their young into the pampas.
The word as explanation, incarnadine, for
our subsequent collusive passions. Because
first there must have been tiered angels
in chorus above the blue globe
spinning its net of lights. Earth
before Man. Life before Birth.
The riddle of the metaphor remains;
the conceiving body conceived in the mind.

III

We're snowed in. And the vast prairie blurs
into a horizon so remote that even
the building we're huddled in can't
break the line into human perspective.
The already burdened roofs whiten into
drifts, become a sod pocked by reindeer
who leap from cloud to tundra soundlessly.
The white sky darkens, a cotton-batting
obscuring stars, but a sift of light
from the hospital helicopter brings us
back into the century. We could
track letters in the snow, should it
come to that. We could make the word
and it would be read.

IV

Once again the day shifts. The poem you
think you have been writing disappears
back into the pen, the day sucked back
into inanition as if the blanket of winter
had at last been secured around you.
Cold at the fingertips, the pen cold,
though the baby kicks over its small
furnace, the radiance rising in indigestive
gulps above the abdomen, lodged there
like an ice-ball, hot and cold at once.
What a blaze of reassurance in this acid!
The small bitterness a leavening, the catalyst
for a joy so fierce it rattles the windows,
dislodges the first shelf of snow from the ledge.

V

Then a stink of burnt plastic—the hair dryer's
coil arcing blue and gold to the faucet
in a synesthetic rainbow stink. And the stink
of argument from the house into the garage
where snow chains lie buried somewhere
in a rusted litter, unfindable, tethering
us to the secular world. No midnight
mass and witnessing of the mystery.
At the far end of the cul-de-sac, carolers
are beginning O Holy Night to the snowed-
in, soundless world of shut houses and cars
planted in crazy eights along embankments
and drives. Across the glare ice and black
skies, in electric sibilance, Silent Night.

VI

From God, our idea of God, the first gift.
But struggling through the morning drifts,
clumsy and laden with packages, we see
ourselves not as images of grace but as
stopped Darwinian evolutes, so poorly
adapted to this world we sink below the crust
at every step. We are ill-prepared for
our part in the miracle. Except there is
the kingdom of the bells, and the dung-
smells of the stable, and the insubstantial
element that finds its way through our boot-
seams and scarves—a winter breath as sudden
as the stillness after a cry, the Christ child
brought to the breast and sleeping there.

IV

Devolution of the Nude

In Whitman's day there were the secret bathers
spied on by his poem's spinster, yearning
behind the glass, in Emerson's day and
Thoreau's, in the Utopian societies eager to
transmute the dross of Puritanism into the gold
of burnished flesh; in every century or half-
century there have been faddists who know
the six openings of the body must go
unstoppered, that the distinction between man
and woman is holy, and the expulsion
from the garden was the garment district's
first advertisement ploy.
                              In our day
there are perhaps fewer of these: acid rain
and factory seepage combine to forecast another
ice-age (this time the glacier greens with alloys),
have made stoppering hygienic;
and we've discovered in place of the open
the principle of the closed—the Victorian tenet
that covered is more alluring than bare,
that Shame's the secret passageway
to Eros. And though we may laugh at Marianne
Moore's remark—"I like the nude," she said,
handing back Kenneth Clark's book, "but
in moderation"—it is us
                              we find
swathed in bedclothes, as if we were asthmatic
invalids under covers calming ourselves
with penlights and turn-of-the-century novels
whose characters' cumbersome cloaks
and flannel layers protect them, protect *us*,
from what is only whispered of: the difficult

birth in the back room, the laying out
of the dead in the parlor, the two occasions
for nakedness that are dreadful
and not for our eyes,

                       not yet.

Ann Lee

—*founder of the First Church of the Millennium (Shakers)*

A serenity so arduously maintained, and at such
frightful cost (but one needn't consider
that anymore), the soul could at last unbend
and become the female Christ, sanctified
in the company of glossy fruit in a plain bowl
and the unadorned cherrywood sconce
holding a single candle, everything "in the neatest
conceivable style," reported the *Richmond Virginia
Inquirer* in 1825. And the superlative
of neat conceiving was precisely the point.
After four hemorrhaging births, the children
all lost in infancy, and a brute husband,
she left for America, leaving behind abhorrent
intercourse—"the flesh consumed upon my bones
and bloody sweat pressed through the pores
of my skin"—and was revealed to be
the celibate divine.
                              Done with blood,
with semen, with the torn body of penetration
and delivery, she was at last the spiritual
mother of painless ghost-children
who would live forever in shining separate
houses. Where there had been coal dust
and stinking mill effluent, there was lemon
oil and lye-scrubbed boards.
Where there had been the rags of aspiring
gentility—lace trimmings, or High Church
embroideries the poor cleaned themselves
to look at but couldn't touch—there was
the planed surface, whitewashed walls, pegs

to hang the chairs on. No altar, or gold,
or carvings. And she, the Manchester slum
girl, could for the first time in her life
simply rest.
                It was better than death.
It was death-in-life.
The body clean, the room clean, the mind
could be drawn out of grossness and float
over the beautifully, artfully rock-tumbled
fences into the acres of immaculate pasture.
The shakings and hallucinations, the leadership
quarrels and canvassing for converts, all
the business of religion, came full-force later,
when she was too far gone into her light-flooded
mind to assume corporeal form.
She had been matter. Now she was essence.
She had spent four crucifixions, had been
impaled on the sex of brutish inevitability,
her daily round had been the Gethsemane
of alleys and verminous warrens.
                       And now
was the peace that passeth understanding.
The congress of the elect, the Lost Tribe
of Israel, Joseph Smith, and Chief
Nez Percé, American History stalking
through the dining hall like a poltergeist,
impregnating the prettiest girls, spiking
the scurvy-curing double lemon pies
with aphrodisiac and psychotropic dust—
all that was still to come. Civil War
was still to come. The Kentucky
settlement would be set upon by soldiers

from both sides, the best horses and men
conscripted, and only the elderly left
who would die out, prisoners of the body
after all.
She could, perhaps, foresee it.
She could no longer care about it.
The message had been conceived and delivered
and she was finished. A legacy
of furniture, some boxy buildings, and
tiny separate beds: all she amounted to
was in the end all she wished to leave.
To see God in a plain room,
to fix serenity in a single bed . . .
The principle was sound
                              and would come round again.

Epilogue

In *Roe v. Wade* the young woman known
as Roe had her baby after all,

the Supreme Court decision came too late
for her, though the kindly black wings

of interpretation rose into a sky
of individual sovereignty for thousands,

millions, afterward. Now in a new afterward
Roe is casting off her pseudonym, despite

car bombings and death threats, to look
for that daughter. She wants to tell her

something. And I wonder how many of us
have been imagining that conversation,

wondering where it would begin.
With fear, but drawing inevitably

toward love? Or is abstraction too easy
here, too open to interpretation

and substitution; *cowardice*, say,
or *oblivion*. It's a poor medium

made poorer by the gross demands
of the body (made by love, we're told,

and fear and carnal oblivion)
whose every hunger enters the ledger

I'm too cowardly to look into. How many
spirits can be dandled on the knee of God,

how many souls inspiriting the hands
of the just; is it matter or energy

that can't be destroyed and does that mean
the amount is fixed, infinity

consisting then of endless repetition,
something I can almost comprehend; would Roe

say that? Would Roe say the soul
that is you would have been born anyway,

even if I'd aborted the body,
and what would the daughter say?

How could either of them bear to say
anything? What new language must there be

when a monument, a landmark,
decides at last to finish the story?

Going Back

What a stage set it seems now,
ironwork crimped around shop
windows in the Louisiana version
of genteel, a smear
of cats moving in diagonals

across the empty street.
Something, the wind perhaps,
is picking through trash
scuttled against the aluminum
grates that blink in synchrony

with the scuddy, gibbous moon,
and it's almost romantic,
as if a tryst were again
being scripted, and it is your
seventeen-year-old self

about to enter. Nothing
in this town has changed—
the actual street is actually
here—but the visual memory blurs.
What the body remembers is not

night, mist, boy coming slowly
forward. What the body
remembers is itself—the blood
a whiskey trail of warmth
extinguished and revived again

and again in the febrile course
of waiting. How long you stood
on this corner before the night
signaled its heart-stopping
yes or *no* is impossible,

from this distance, to imagine.
You stood. Eventually,
you moved, and the universe
ratcheted back on its dolly
tracking you, drawing its line

across your palm,
which I look into now, as into
an inverse lens, to see the girl
before the expulsion,
before the love story begins.

Safety

October approaches with its first boxcar
of winey air; the trees' red galaxies

crazing the squirrels
as summer uncouples and chuffs away.

Here, the suburbs begin their winter
soups and bread, kitchen smells

leaking out into the abandoned playgrounds
whose swift intrigues

and configurations of exclusion and grace
dissolve in the brothy call to home.

And now every house intoxicates,
every sweater is the promise of frost

and frost the promise of jack-o'-lantern—
Is this a vision? That fire in the skull

an approachable terror? If not in the grin,
then not in the shadows. If not in the hallway,

then not under the bed . . .
Does the mind send out its own half-

illumined cars, any one of which can carry
us to those dim but beckoning far Octobers?

The car of left-alone, the car of best
costume, French kiss? Then I choose

the farthest one, the one with the guard-
rail and platform from which you can watch

the ghouls receding. The one I think that he
is on, and I can meet him there.

Of Serious Conversation

—what's left to be said?
That it was a way to leave the party

and find our way past the drunken cars
floating down the street. Or it was

the tongue suggesting itself to the ear,
the pocket of night inviting the hand in,

and yes it's good to delay the moment
of flesh for the moment of ideas, especially

under this moon starved of light and
thinned into infinity because we want it

that way, a vast bath of pathos draining
over the backyard's sorrowing frogs.

Oh it's good to be done with self-improvement,
to let the mind and body inch

back to flannel. Inside, Flaubert is dozing,
and the Russians—who would rave if we'd

let them—have split from their Livres
des Poches and it's good to ignore them,

good to be outside researching the quiddity
of good, splitting the hair of distinction

finer and finer until it is that starveling
darkling hooked up in the tree.

Barbie's Ferrari

Nothing is quite alien or quite recognizable at this speed,
Though there is the suggestion of curve, a mutant
Curvature designed to soften or offset
The stiletto toes and karate arms that were too
Angular for her last car, a Corvette as knifed as Barbie
Herself, and not the blood-red of Italian Renaissance.
This is Attention. This is detail fitted to sheer
Velocity. For her knees, after all, are locked—
Once fitted into the driving pit, she can only accelerate
Into a future that becomes hauntingly like the past:
Nancy Drew in her yellow roadster, a convertible,
I always imagined, the means to an end
Almost criminal in its freedom, its motherlessness.
For Barbie, too, is innocent of parents, pressing
Her unloved breasts to the masculine wheel, gunning
The turn into the hallway and out over the maiming stairs,
Every jolt slamming her uterus into uselessness, sealed,
Sealed up and preserved, everything about her becoming
Pure Abstraction and the vehicle for Desire: to be Nancy,
To be Barbie, to feel the heaven of Imagination
Breathe its ether on your cheeks, rosying in the slipstream
As the speedster/roadster/Ferrari plummets over the rail
Into the ocean of waxed hardwood below. To crash and burn
And be retrieved. To unriddle the crime. To be
Barbie with a plot! That's the soulful beauty of it.
That's the dreaming child.
Not the dawn of Capital, or the factories of Hong Kong
Reversing the currency in Beijing. Not the ovarian moon
In eclipse. Just the dreaming child, the orphan,
Turning in slow motion in the air above the bannister,
For whom ideas of gender and marketplace are nothings
Less than nothing. It's the car she was born for.
It's Barbie you mourn for.

Utopian Turtletop

The car was finally named Edsel,
Turtletop being perhaps too diffident, and Utopian
    unrealizable, and therefore expensive,
        and a gracious Marianne Moore

conceded to a gallant Henry Ford.
There was no more to it, but the thrill of speculation:
    think how vibrant, if only for the space
        of one selling season,

the conjunction of art and commerce
could have been! For poets to read into machinery
    the essential, even mystically arrived at,
        name; for the magnates,

the giants of steel, to actually
consider it . . . But that of course would've been
    wholly Utopian, or worse, caricature
        perpetrated in tricorn and cape

flapping about at the prow
of an Edsel ramming itself straight into billboard
    Americana. Merely a flashier demise.
        But the fault

may not have lain
solely in the product. There exists an English
    purveyor, of high Romantic mien,
        who markets sexual aids

under the titles "Prelude"
and "The Excursion" and (this is certainly a bit
    of public school erudition),
        "This Living Hand,"

whose advertisements
at certain London subway stops seem evidence
    of continuous and lucrative
        production.

    So perhaps it's a cultural
distinction, British wit as opposed to American
    humor, for the products themselves
        share an affinity,

    a sleekness, say, or taste
for acceleration, an indulgence in fantasy
    that Edsel didn't satisfy. It wasn't
        American enough, or, rather,

    was too much the Ed-at-
the-hardware-store version of American, not
    glamorous or passionate. And while
        Turtletop would have been

    far worse—death
on the showroom floor—the ludicrous does seem
    closer somehow to our national
        self-definition,

    for who reads poetry now?
or would recognize allusion in the service
    of mechanical ecstasy? Maybe
        we are poorer for that.

    Maybe the wildness of
language, even at the absurd level of automobiles,
    could have done a positive good,
        sent someone back

to the poems, as perhaps
the sordid posters send some Londoners back
to Wordsworth and Keats. Nevertheless,
that there was, for a moment,

on a paper sketch, Utopian
Turtletop, is heartening: Once upon a time a poet
named a car. And the American Dream
grew larger.

Wuthering Heights

After so many wind-
swept versions, it's hard to see across
the intervening years
back to the original: cloaked in his dangerous
dignity, obsessor, dog-hanger,
his hands on the woman's throat, in love
(yes, but *on the throat*); even Hollywood,
which made him Beautiful,
even Movietone, which made him Despair, couldn't quite mask
the acid that was Heathcliff.

I wanted them both out of the picture.
I wanted the dog back.
Ghosting the moors was, at the end,
rather too good for them, a kind of heaven,
as Dante's third circle is,
the circularity of obsession rounding
back always to the first point.
Heathcliff-who-is-Cathy-who-is-Heathcliff,
and everyone around them suffering.

Even Emily. "Having formed
these beings," Charlotte wrote, "she did
not know what she had done, but shuddered
under the grinding influence of natures
so relentless, so lost and fallen."
But this is much like the pot calling
the kettle black, as both sisters
thrilled to the writing of "certain
vivid and fearful scenes" that kept them
up at night. Something in these two
loved Heathcliff, at least so long
as their brother lived, "a brief, erring,

suffering, feverish life." It was *his* death
that killed off Heathcliff,
all his vices dissolved, or translated
into a clarifying woe, and Emily stricken
with a pain in her heart and lungs
from which she never recovered.
Mrs. Gaskell records the last days,
the pang Charlotte felt when,
having searched the hollows and crevices
of the moors for a lingering spray
of heather, "just one spray
however withered," to take in to Emily,
she saw it wasn't recognized
by the dim and different eyes.
The heath flower, its pink spikes
disappearing over the cliff,
over the abyss that Heathcliff was,
had lost its power for her. She died
not knowing what she'd done.

I keep a spike of heather, immortalized
in lucite, as a paperweight
on my desk. It is, in a way, my charm,
my reminder that what Heathcliff embodies
is not love, that what Cathy is
is not love, and that what first drew me
in my husband—his blackness, his obsessive
and absolute sex, his hauteur—
isn't the whole story. There is
that other secret about him
that isn't Heathcliff, that other

nineteenth-century virtue ill-defined by
but containing all those moral
abstractions: charity, serenity, love—
which Romance only deracinates
and obscures.

ABOUT THE AUTHOR

Lynne McMahon is an associate professor of English at the University of Missouri, Columbia. Her first book of poems, *Faith,* was published in 1988.

COLOPHON

Devolution of the Nude was designed and typeset by Scott-Martin Kosofsky at The Philidor Company, Boston. The types are Montaigne Sabon, a new version of Jan Tschichold's Sabon created by Mr. Kosofsky for a new edition of the *Autobiography of Michel de Montaigne*, and Weiss Italic, the well-known design of the esteemed early twentieth-century calligrapher Emil Rudolf Weiss. The headbands and cover artwork, inspired by Joseph Cornell's collage, were made in Adobe Photoshop. The book was composed in Quark XPress, entirely in the PostScript language. The book was printed and bound by Haddon Craftsmen, Scranton, Pennsylvania.